Charlie,

To a very dear man.

I miss comparing

stories with you.

Martha

Real Life Monsters

by

Martha Dickson Allen

PRENTICE-HALL, INC.

ENGLEWOOD CLIFFS, NEW JERSEY

*To Cathy and to David. To my two
little inspirations, Scott and Jason.
And especially to John.*

REAL LIFE MONSTERS
Copyright © 1978 by Martha Dickson Allen

Printed in the United States of America

Prentice-Hall International, Inc., London
Prentice-Hall of Australia, Pty. Ltd., North Sydney
Prentice-Hall of Canada, Ltd., Toronto
Prentice-Hall of India Private Ltd., New Delhi
Prentice-Hall of Japan, Inc., Tokyo
Prentice-Hall of Southeast Asia Pte. Ltd., Singapore

10 9 8 7 6 5 4 3 2 1

Library of Congress Cataloging in Publication Data

Allen, Martha Dickson,
    Real life monsters.

    Bibliography: p.
    Includes index.
    SUMMARY: Describes the discovery of three
animals once thought to be imaginary (the
gorilla, Komodo dragon, and giant squid) and
discusses the research being conducted to prove or
disprove the existence of the Loch Ness Monster,
Big Foot, and the Abominable Snowman.
    1. Animals—Miscellanea—Juvenile literature.
2. Monsters—Juvenile literature. [1. Animals—Miscellanea. 2. Monsters] I. Title.
QL49.G29   001.9'44   78-6985
ISBN 0-13-766568-7

DO YOU BELIEVE IN MONSTERS?

Do you believe in monsters?

Have you ever seen one?

Monsters appear in fairy tales, legends, and folklore of peoples throughout history. They are living among us to-day. And some may yet be out there in our world, still to be discovered.

For hundreds and thousands of years, many people have seen manlike hairy giants roaming jungles, forests, and high mountain regions of the world. Others have been terrified of giant crocodiles, sea snakes, and water monsters. Some of these creatures have been captured and identified. Others still manage to elude us.

In 1917, Baron Georges Cuvier, the French naturalist, announced that all the world's animals had been found. But since this naive and premature judgment, we have discovered the giant panda, the wide-lipped rhinoceros, the coelacanth (a prehistoric fish), the okapi (related to the giraffe), the spotted zebra, the white giraffe, a new species of shark, and several of the animals mentioned in this book, to name only a few. Every year, in fact, based on a National Geographic Society report, it is estimated that scientists discover and classify 15 new reptiles or amphibians, 50 new mammals, 100 new fish, 15 new birds, and at least 5,000 new insects.

In this book we will discuss animals that exist today, but which for many reasons, had remained a mystery to mankind for as long as 2500 years. We will also learn about several animals whose existence is still questioned by scientists, although there is strong evidence that they, too, inhabit our world. If these elusive creatures are ever found we will have made one of the most important discoveries of the century, perhaps in all of history.

TABLE OF CONTENTS

THE GORILLA

A silver bowl, found 700 years before Christ, records that the Phoenicians may have been the first people to discover the ape. Depicted on the bowl are scenes from a hunt in the African mountains showing a hairy apelike figure, about to throw a rock.

1

Some 250 years later, Hanno, an admiral in the fleet of Carthage, sailed out of the Mediterranean Sea to explore the Atlantic coast of Africa. At a bay called the Southern Horn he came upon an island "full of savage people, the greater part of whom were women, whose bodies were hairy and whom our interpreters called Gorillae. Though we pursued the men, we could not seize any of them; but all fled from us, escaping over precipes, and defending themselves with stones. Three women were taken, however, but they attacked their conductors with their teeth and hands and could not be prevailed on to accompany us. Having killed them we flayed them, and brought their skins to Carthage."

The skins were still there when the Romans later destroyed the city of Carthage, but they soon disappeared. No one had understood what kind of beings had lived within those hairy skins. Some believed that they had belonged to a race of barbarians. African tribes believed the gorillas were bad men who had been turned into hairy animals by witch doctors. Others thought that they were just lazy people pretending to be animals so they wouldn't have to work. Some even thought gorillas could talk but were afraid to for fear of being captured and sold as slaves. But most people doubted that such animals could be living in their time and be unknown to science.

There is no word of the gorilla again until the fifteenth century when they were mentioned in European literature. However, by the mid-1800s evidence began to appear, signs that the hairy animals had indeed existed. In 1846, a missionary to Africa sent a skull to a doctor in Boston. Drawings of the skull were then sent to the Royal

College of Surgeons in London. After a second skeleton arrived in Philadelphia, excitement grew and a search was finally organized to find the mysterious beast. In 1854, the Philadelphia Academy of Natural Sciences found a young explorer willing to solve the 2500-year riddle.

Paul DuChaillu, a French-American, was only twenty-five years old when he embarked upon this adventure. His father had been a trader on the West Coast of Africa and Paul had spent his youth there. However, so little was known about the creature that no one could advise DuChaillu where to begin his search. He chose to enter the country from the coast of the Gabun, a territory near the equator. It was the beginning of what became a four-year exploration.

African members of his search party insisted that the mysterious animals's habitat was in the deepest, densely forested regions of the jungle. So, for endless weeks, DuChaillu and his men battled thick vines and vegetation, swamps, and huge boulders. They braved the most rugged wilderness in Africa to seek out the world's "last" unknown animal.

Detail from Phoenician bowl.

After walking 8000 miles and crossing three mountain ranges, food supplies were completely exhausted, so the men began roasting monkeys on coals and eating them. For some time the forest had begun to grow strangely silent, with only birds calling and monkeys chattering to break the stillness. After days of silence the men heard thrashing noises—sounds of twigs snapping and branches breaking—and then the woods were suddenly filled with a tremendous barking roar. As the men moved quietly forward, they could see a great beast breaking down small trees. When they moved closer, the beast, who had been moving about on all fours, stood up tall in front of them. DuChaillu recalled:

> *He looked at us boldly in the face. He stood about a dozen yards from us, and was a sight I think never to forget. Nearly six feet high, with immense body, huge chest, great muscular arms . . . fiercely glaring, large deep-grey eyes, and a hellish expression of face, it seemed to me some nightmare vision.*

That moment, in 1856 was the first time any American or European had seen the lowland gorilla, which DuChaillu called the "king of the African forest."

> *He was not afraid of us. He stood there and beat his breast with huge fists till it resounded like an immense bass drum, which is their mode of offering defiance, meantime giving vent to roar after roar.*
>
> *His eyes began to flash fiercer fire as we stood motionless on the defensive and the crest of short hair on his forehead began to twitch rapidly up and down, while his powerful fangs were shown as he again sent*

forth a thunderous roar. He reminded me of nothing but of some hellish dream-creature, half-man, half-beast, which old artists pictured in representations of the infernal regions. He advanced a few steps then stopped to utter that hideous roar again—advanced again, and finally stopped at about six yards from us. And here, just as he began another of his roars, beating his breast in rage, we fired and killed him.

Although DuChaillu brought back remains of seventeen gorilla specimens, some skeptics still doubted the animal's existence. However, soon the body of another gorilla was sent to the British Museum. And other explorers began to find more gorillas.

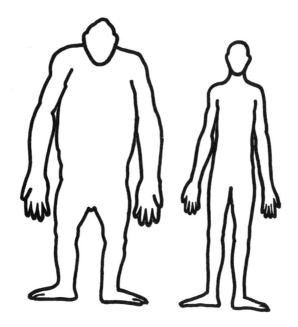

Comparison of size of a gorilla and a human.

In time, gorillas were living in zoos all over the United States and Europe. M'Bongo, whose home was the San Diego Zoo, grew to be over 8 feet tall. Makoto, of the Bronx Zoo, lived to be 11 years old. The captured animals established that gorillas could exceed 6 feet in height and weigh over 500 pounds.

How did gorillas escape detection until 1856? Even today there is very little skeletal evidence that gorillas exist. The jungle is so thick and the ground so moist that bodies decay at a rapid rate. Most skeletons, we suspect, are eaten by other animals, the clean-up crew of the jungle.

Gorillas are very shy and can quickly detect the presence of a human being. They have an ability to disappear without being seen or heard and without leaving a trace of their presence. This trait kept the largest of the great apes, the mountain gorilla, a mystery until the twentieth century. A German explorer finally located the beast in 1902 near the Congo basin, a thousand miles east of any area where gorillas had ever been found. Famous explorers had wandered all over mountain gorilla country for more than fifty years yet none had met its most prominent inhabitant. Scientists suspect that still another species of gorilla exists. Skins and skeletons were found prior to 1913 of what has been called the pygmy gorilla, but it has never been seen by man.

Gorillas are peaceful, leisurely animals who lead the life of wanderers. Although leopards sometimes kill young gorillas, this occurs very rarely. Their only natural enemy is man. Gorillas sleep fifteen hours a day and hike a half mile each day. The males are never seen fighting, although they have been seen with wounds about the eyes, which suggest that they do occasionally come to blows. When a companion dies the others cover its body with grass and leaves.

They feed on fruit and vegetation and get their moisture from their food. When thirsty, they soak the fur on the backs of their hands and suck it, for they have an aversion to water. They are afraid to cross even small streams. This fear limits their wanderings considerably and permits zoos to contain gorillas in designated areas by surrounding them with moats.

Contrary to DuChaillu's thinking, gorillas beat their chests to relieve tension. They are gentle creatures, but both sexes, after growing to be about one year old, beat their chests. Males will also put on quite a show by roaring, rising on hindlegs, running sideways, and tossing vegetation into the air. This is meant to terrify us, but is usually a bluff. An actual attack is quite rare. The male may chase an intruder who runs away, even biting and scratching him. But gorilla-hunting tribes consider it a disgrace to be wounded by a gorilla, for this means that the man was running away at the time. Unprovoked attacks are unheard of.

When male gorillas are ten years old they grow silver hairs on their backs and one becomes leader of the group.

Silverback males will glare at young gorillas or slap the ground if they are too noisy or play too roughly. When females start screaming at each other, the leader glares at them and they calm down quickly. When the leader wants quiet, he gets quiet. When a silverback male pulls a leaf from a plant and puts it between his lips, watch out—it's a signal that he is going to get violent. But the leader is also gentle with his family. Females nestle against him and babies crawl all over his huge body. Gorillas like to build nests in the trees and on the ground. Sometimes when they build nests on a hillside, during the night, they roll out and down the hill in their sleep.

Young gorillas have been kept as pets, a relationship that can be difficult. The young are subject to the same tantrums and rowdiness as human children, the difference being that they are much stronger and therefore more destructive. They need constant attention and affection, and if their favorite person is gone the young gorilla will pout, refuse to eat, become sick, and may even die. Zoo keepers sometimes provide television sets for the adults to watch and often play with young gorillas to keep them from being lonely.

THE GIANT SQUID

We have always been fascinated by
the sea and lured by its many
mysteries. Its waters have
provided the cradle of
life and in its dark
recesses live some
of the strangest
creatures on earth,
many surely still
unseen by man. Lurking in
the deepest parts of the sea is
a monster of gigantic proportions,
known in Scandinavian folklore as
the kraken. Once thought to be
a myth, there is still much
about this masterpiece of sea
life that is a mystery to scientists.

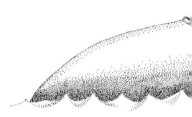

King Sverre of Norway first used the word, kraken, in the twelfth century, to describe a sea monster. Later it came to mean a giant squid or octopus. Originally the old Norse word was applied to any large unknown animal of the sea. Finally it was used to identify any one of the more than 350 known species of giant squid. Today kraken again means a fabulous Scandinavian sea monster.

The label, giant squid, includes the class of Cephalopoda such as the cuttlefish, nautilus, squid, octopus, kraken, and any other marine animal that moves by expelling water through a siphon, has eight to ten arms, highly developed eyes, and jaws with a sharp beak.

A bishop in Norway saw a giant squid in 1755 and called it a sea snake. Early stories told of giant squids raising their frightful heads from the water and snapping men out of

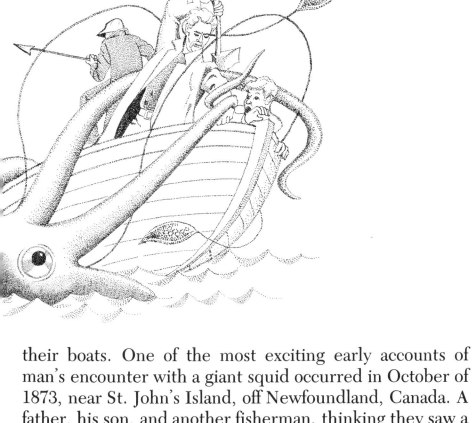

their boats. One of the most exciting early accounts of man's encounter with a giant squid occurred in October of 1873, near St. John's Island, off Newfoundland, Canada. A father, his son, and another fisherman, thinking they saw a boat's sail in the water, rowed closer and struck it with a gaff. The object responded violently to the men's curious poke, and a giant squid reared its enormous beak, striking the boat, while two huge arms encircled the gunwale. One of the men cut off the two arms with an ax. At this, the creature retreated rapidly, discharging an inky fluid that darkened the water for 200 to 300 yards. As it held its tail high in the air, the men could see its body and estimated it to be 60 feet long and 10 feet across. The severed arms of the monster provided proof that the kraken was no longer only a myth.

Because the arms of the giant squid, without distortion, can assume a serpent's head, it is possible that they were the "sea snakes" reported by ship's crews in the nineteenth century. Or perhaps these sailors were really seeing giant eels, or manta rays; (the latter sometimes reach the monstrous weight of 3000 pounds.) In any case, the giant squid is monster enough for most of us. It is the largest animal without a backbone or skeleton, and the most ferocious.

Squids live in seas and oceans all over the world, some at upper levels near the surface, others as deep down as a mile. The smallest squids measure less than an inch long. The giant measures over 70 feet. Very few giant squids have ever been found alive at the ocean's surface. They prefer to live in the deepest parts of the sea and are only sighted at the surface when sick or when locked in mortal combat with a whale who has come up to breathe. A sea captain cruising off the eastern tip of Brazil in 1875 witnessed just such a spectacle through binoculars. He saw "a monstrous sea serpent coiled twice round a large sperm whale. . . . The serpent whirled its victim round and round for about fifteen minutes, and then suddenly dragged the whale to the bottom, head first."

Whaling men often see the imprint of squid suckers in the hide of sperm whale. Measurements of scars carried by captured whales indicate that the attacking squids have attained a length of up to 120 feet. The whale is usually the victor, however, because the toothless beak of the giant squid is unable to penetrate the tough hide and blubber of the whale. As a result, parts of the bodies of giant squid are often found in the stomachs of whales captured at sea.

Over the years, specimens of giant squid, 30 to 50 feet long, have been seen, dead or dying, floating on the water's edge, or stranded on beaches. In the decade of 1870–1880, there were 55 to 60 of these animals sighted by fishermen in the sea off Newfoundland. No one has ever been able to explain why so many appeared at that time and at that particular place. Maybe there was a shift in their food sources, or maybe submarines drove them toward the shore where they are not usually found. However, to find a specimen today is a rare occurrence, but they do exist. At the present time, there are no living specimens for anyone to see.

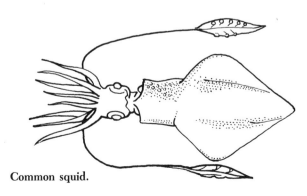

Common squid.

The most frightening part of the giant squid's strange pulpy lump of a body is the head. The eyes are huge giant lenses, up to 15 inches in diameter, over twice the size of the eyes of the blue whale. They are very much like the eyes of mammals and are positioned on the head so that the squid can see backward and forward. Inside the eyeballs are light-producing organs, which permit the squid to illuminate the objects it wants to see.

In front of those eyes the face separates into eight long, boneless arms, each feeling out into the sea for more victims. Squids have eight arms like an octopus, but as a bonus, they have two tentacles, which octopuses do not have. The tentacles are always longer than the arms and are used for darting and grasping a victim. The oval blade on each end makes the tentacle look like a long-handled teaspoon. These tentacles shoot out and seize a victim, then draw it into the grasp of the arms, where it is held while the animal's deadly beak tears it apart. The beak of a squid resembles a parrot's beak and is located in the center, surrounded by arms. It is so strong it can tear chunks out of wood. Sucking discs on the arms and tentacles of the giant squid are encircled with 50 or more sharp teeth. Wartlike structures on both tentacle can interlock, combining the strength of two tentacles to draw in an especially strong prey.

Like the octopus, the squid has a muscular covering over its body called the mantle. Beneath this mantle lies a hornlike brace, or shell, called the pen, which can be over four feet long in the giant.

At times these animals seem almost jet-propelled. At the back of the body is a long tail shaped like the tip of a spear, and a special navigating organ in the head helps them zero in on a target with the accuracy of a torpedo. They can maneuver better than the octopus and can execute swift sharp turns. Nature has truly provided the giant squid with all the necessary equipment to become a terrifyingly efficient killing machine.

Squids feed on plankton, sometimes microscopic in size, and smaller fish like the mackerel. However, they are also cannibalistic and will eat their own kind. The squid has two speeds—fast and slow. He travels forward at slow speeds by the movement of fins. However, when he attacks, he propels himself backward on a zigzag course until he nears grasping range. Then he quickly turns and shoots forward like a living arrow while his tentacles flick out to seize his prey. This sea pirate will attack whole schools of fish, satisfy his hunger, then continue to kill, as a shark does, becoming more and more excited and bloodthirsty in his killing frenzy.

The nervous system of squids reacts almost instantly to fear or hunger. As a result, the animals can drive their bodies to escape or to attack in a second. Large squids take in water at one end and shoot it out the other through their siphon with the force of a fire hose. They are the most powerful of all spineless swimmers and can propel their rocket-shaped bodies through the sea at a lightning pace.

There are many tales of squids attacking boats and snatching away members of the crew. Once a giant squid attacked a man who had wandered into the shallow water of an inlet cave. Also, many stories tell of seamen and sea travelers having landed on what they thought were small islands, only to find the land begin to writhe beneath them. There are versions that tell of crew members disembarking from their ships to cook a meal on land. However, the heat from the cook fires so disturbed the animal that it reared its huge back, turned over and forced the crews to flee back to their vessels nearby.

Captain Jean Magus Dens was a well-known and respected mariner. After making several voyages to China as a master trader, he retired and settled in Dunkirk. It is said that whenever he had the opportunity he would tell the story of a voyage he made from Saint Helena (off the African Coast) to Cape Negro (in the Mediterranean). One day he was becalmed and took advantage of the forced idleness of his crew to have the sides of the vessel scraped and painted. As three of his men were standing on planks hung over the side, an enormous cuttle rose from the water and threw one of its arms around two of the sailors, whom it tore away, along with the scaffolding on which they stood. With another arm it seized the third man, who held tightly to the rigging and shouted for help. Although his shipmates cut away the creature's arm with axes and knives, the seaman became delirious and died the following night.

Another story tells of a giant squid that took an entire ship into its grasp. One night the squid climbed onto the side of the ship and the captain found the ends of its tentacles along the deck. One tentacle grasped the ship's stern. Then the captain walked to the other end of the ship and there he saw the end of another tentacle. The ship was 175 feet long!

One of the largest of recorded giant squids washed up on a beach in 1924. The body was 9 feet thick. That is higher than the ceiling of an average room. Scientists believe this specimen was more than 200 feet long, not including its two long tentacles. It might well have stretched through the sea for a distance two thirds as long as a football field!

Because of an incident on the island of Jamaica, in the late 1800s, we are provided with a glimpse of the breeding habits of giant squid, habits still largely a mystery to man. Children playing on the Jamaican beach found a large strange object stranded above the tide line. Excitedly they cried to their father that they had found a huge "sausage." Their father, a scientist, recognized the object as an egg case of a giant squid. It was five to six feet long and about as big around as a milking pail.

When squid are ready to mate, one of the arms of the male grows longer and larger and changes into a reproductive organ. He uses the special arm to place a packet of sperm beneath the mantle of the female, where the eggs become fertilized. The female squid does not guard her eggs after they hatch.

For some species of squid, mating is the final act of their lives. Tired, weak, and often wounded by fights during courtship, the parents wait feebly to die. But as life is ending for them, new life emerges from the eggs left behind. And another generation of squids is born to speed through the sea, prey upon their neighbors, grow, reproduce, and in their turn, die.

21

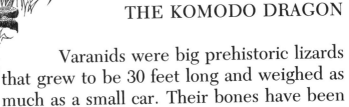

THE KOMODO DRAGON

Varanids were big prehistoric lizards
that grew to be 30 feet long and weighed as
much as a small car. Their bones have been
found in such places as Wyoming and
Australia, and yet they have been dead for
60 million years. Or have they?

In the twentieth century, who would have
thought we would ever see
the dragons we read
about in myths or perhaps
dreamed of in our nightmares?
Sixty million years had passed, and
we felt safe from such creatures.
We believed that the closest things
to dragons were six-foot-long

23

lizards that lived in tropical America, the West Indies, and the Galapagos islands—lizards known as iguanas.

But, in the early 1900s, a disturbing story came from the East Indies in the far Pacific when a pilot with plane trouble was forced to land on the island known as Komodo. He came back telling of the dragons that had made his stay on Komodo a nightmare. No one believed him.

In 1912, before the pilot's terrifying experience, a man had presented a lizard's skin to the director of a small museum on Java. The specimen was from the island of Komodo. The museum director recognized it as a varanid skin and sent his own men to Komodo, who then returned with other specimens. The American Museum of Natural History heard of the findings and sent a team to investigate. W. Douglas Burden, his wife, and a party of three, traveled 12,000 miles to see their first dragon.

Komodo Island is one of the most dangerous places in all the world for on its soil are found all four orders of poisonous snakes known to mankind, and the world's largest lizard. Rain forests and tall grasses cover the hilly earth and jagged mountain peaks resembling gigantic sharp teeth make the island seem like the perfect setting for the home of the giant dragon monster.

In 1927 Burden wrote:

> *I saw my first dragon lizard in the open. He was a monster—huge and hoary . . . the lizard was working his way slowly down from the mountain crags. The sun slanted down the hill, so that a black shadow preceded the black beast as he came. It was a perfectly marvelous sight—a primeval monster in a primeval setting— sufficient to give any hunter a real thrill.*

He would lower his head, flash a long yellow bifur-
cated (forked) tongue into the air, and then move read-
ily toward the bait . . . in the process of gorging him-
self, the long sharp claws are used indiscriminately to
scrape and tear with, while the thin, recurved teeth
with serrated edges are employed to rip off great
chunks of the foul meat. On one occasion, a lizard
swallowed the whole hind-quarters of a boar at one
gulp—hoofs, legs, hams, vertebrae, and all.

Burden also saw the dragon stand up on its hind legs, like dinosaurs were known to do. He captured several live dragons and took them along with some dead ones, back to New York where thousands of people stood in line to see them.

Soon after they were first identified by scientists in 1912, Komodo Dragons came under government protection. Therefore, they are in little danger from man.

Why were Komodo Dragons unknown to the world until 1912? Simply because no one lived on Komodo and no one ever visited the remote island except for an occasional fisherman hunting for pearls or turtles. Then a sultan from a neighboring island began deporting criminals and other undesirables to Komodo. These frightened men told of 23-foot-long ferocious crocodiles, but no one would believe their stories.

How did these prehistoric animals survive? Komodo and other small islands, Rintja, Flores, and Padar, where the dragons have also been found, are located in the midst of a group of Indonesian islands that stretch for 800 miles in the Pacific. Varanid lizards probably swam there from Australia. Their natural enemies, the tiger and the wild dog, were unable to swim that far, and so Komodo became the perfect sanctuary.

Although there are reports of much longer lizards, the official length assigned to the creatures is 10 feet. They can weigh as much as 300 pounds. The body is stout, and somewhat flat, with a long head and short legs. The toes have long claws. The powerful tail is as long again as the body and is used to beat off the young ones when feeding. The mouths of the lizards are red and lined with saw-edged teeth. The young are dark-colored with red circles all over the body and around the neck bands. The latter disappear and only the red circles remain on the gray-brown bodies of adults. When babies hatch, they are 18 inches long. They spend their first year in trees. Sometimes half-grown dragons climb trees but adults cannot because they are too heavy. Young dragons feed on insects, lizards, rodents, birds, and their eggs. When grown, they eat deer, pigs, and monkeys. Once a 110-pound female devoured a 90-pound wild hog in 17 minutes. A Komodo Dragon in the act of devouring prey is a terrifying sight. It attacks water buffalo by darting in and severing an Achilles tendon; then while the animal is helpless, it quickly disembowels it. It even preys on its own kind, which is why its population stays close to 5,000.

Every morning at 8:30, the dragons come out to look for food, which they smell with their constantly flicking tongues. They can smell decayed flesh from a distance of five miles. When eating, they like to gorge themselves and then lie still, sometimes for as long as a week, while digesting the meal. One might expect thunderous noises to emerge from such a beast, but actually the Komodo Dragon makes barely any sound at all. At night they sleep in holes of crevices among the rocks. They may live as long as 100 years.

They are very dangerous animals. They can move as fast as 12.5 miles per hour and have been known to swim 1,000 feet through heavy currents to islets in order to attack tethered goats. Natives will not go near haunts of the giant lizard after dark and are very afraid of them at all other times as well.

A fantasy come to life, the Komodo Dragon has not proved disappointing. Although our real live dragon doesn't breathe fire, like the mythical beasts of old, his long, flicking, yellow forked tongue and armor-like hide make him as formidable as the wildest dragons of our wildest nightmares.

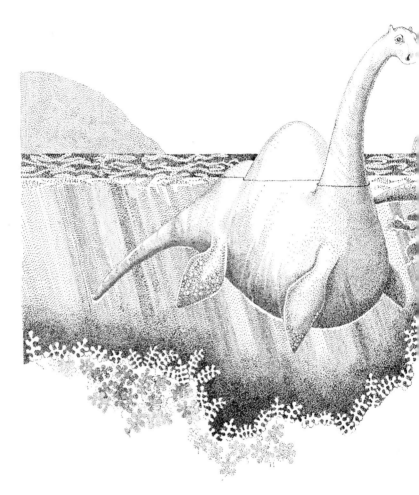

THE LOCH NESS MONSTER

As Saint Columba was crossing the water of Ness one day, he came to a bank where he saw townspeople burying a poor soul who had been killed by a water monster while swimming. Some men in a nearby boat had tried to rescue the hapless victim but were too late to save him from the monster's terrible bite. Saint Columba sent one of his

companions to swim out to the now drifting boat and bring it in to shore. As the man dutifully jumped into the lake to retrieve the boat, the monster, sensing his waters again being disturbed, suddenly emerged and rushed up to the swimmer with a great roar and open mouth. Everyone was terrified. But Saint Columba raised his hand, made the sign of the cross, invoked the name of God, and cried: "Think not to go further nor touch thou that man. Quick! Go back!" The beast, afraid of the holy man, fled backward and sank back down into the depths of the loch. The year was 565 A.D. And the first account of that event is inscribed in the history of St. Benedict's Abbey in Fort Augustus, at the southern tip of the Loch.

Nearly one thousand years later, in 1527, *A History of Scotland* records:

> *This terrible beast issuing out of the water early one morning about mid summer, he did very easily and without any force or straining of himself, overthrow huge oaks with his tail and therewith killed outright three men that hunted him with three strokes of his tail, the rest of them saving themselves in trees thereabouts, whilst the aforesaid monster returned to the loch.*

Although this story is surely exaggerated, the scene is again Loch Ness.

And even though more than 1400 years have passed since the first account of the water monster, people still believe that something lurks in the now famous mountain lake. It is thought to be an ancestor of that first hideous creature, but by comparison, the Loch Ness monster of today seems a curious and gentle beast.

Nessie, or sea horse, as she is affectionately called, plays a large part in the folklore of the Scottish Highlands. Mothers warn their children to keep away from the "terrible water kelpie." However, until 1933, the rest of the world was unaware that a sea monster existed at all, and especially not in a small freshwater lake in the Great Glen of Scotland.

Loch Ness, which villagers often call Locke na Bieste (Lake of the Monster), is not as small as it first appears. Although less than a mile wide, it is 24 miles long and over 970 feet deep. Scientists believe that Loch Ness was once an arm of the sea, cut off from the ocean when land began to rise as a huge glacier pushed its way through during the Ice Age. This catastrophe, over 5,000 years ago, could have caused huge sea beasts to become stranded in the loch. And they could have learned to adapt to freshwater conditions as sharks, seals, and dolphins have been known to do. Since there is a shortage of plants in the loch, Nessie is most likely a meat eater. The abundant supply of large fish found in the Ness could supply more than enough food to sustain several large sea monsters. And there are scientists who believe that as many as 20 to 30 such beasts could presently inhabit the loch, some maybe as much as 100 feet long!

Scotland is not the only haunt of sea monsters, however. They have also been sighted in high mountain lakes of Canada, the United States, and in South America. In the United States these creatures are seen mainly in the lakeland of Wisconsin, the Nebraska plains lakes, and in lakes of several mountain states. There is the Great Sandy Lake Monster of Minnesota, the Lake Erie Monster, and the Flathead Lake Monster of Montana. Idaho, Nevada, Oregon, California, and Utah also report such critters. In 1972, a photograph was taken of a serpent-like creature in Lake Champlain (Vermont). Ontario, Canada, is the home of the Igopogo, and Winnipeg is the address of the Rock Lake Monster. British Columbia has its famous Ogopogo.

At one time *The New York Times* offered a $1,000 reward for a picture of this beast.

In 1977, a picture was taken of a "saltwater Nessie." In April of that year, a Japanese trawler looking for mackerel off the coast of New Zealand hauled up quite a surprise in its fishing nets. The two-ton carcass appeared to be that of a mysterious beast 32 feet long, with a long neck and four flippers. "Some of the crew thought it was a whale, others a turtle without a shell, and some joked that it was a monster," said fishery executive Michihiko Yano, who was on board. After examining photos and sketches of the creature, Japanese marine biologists believed that the monster theory might not be so farfetched. Unfortunately, the experts had no evidence beyond the pictures and a piece of one of the creature's flippers; the crew had thrown the stinking carcass over the side fearing that the fatty fluids oozing from it would spoil the cargo of fish.

The Japanese were embarrassed to have thrown away such a prize, for surely an animal thought to be extinct would have been worth much more than a boatload of tuna. It was assumed that other such monsters might be in the vicinity and soon Soviet trawlers were reported to be steaming toward New Zealand waters. Orders were given to the Japanese crew not to throw back any strange creatures discovered on future voyages.

Back in Scotland, however, we find that Loch Ness does not have a monopoly on sea monsters. In 1969, a creature who could have been Nessie's twin, attacked a boat in Lake Morar, 40 miles from the Ness. Monsters could have actually walked to this lake from the ocean since it is so near the sea. This bad-tempered creature has been named Morar Maggie.

Nessie, however, is the most famous of all water monsters and is seen at least 20 times each year. Eyewitnesses claim she is from 30-50 feet long and has a giraffe-like neck. Some have noticed a fin or crest running down the back of her neck; others describe it as looking like a horse's mane. Her head has been called snakelike, goat-like, horselike, or turtlelike. Some people see her eyes as large and round; others perceive them as slits in a darning needle. Still others report they saw no eyes at all. She has three humps on her back. Her skin is dappled, almost cow-like in appearance, and is the texture of an elephant's skin. She has four fins or flippers and a large, blunt-ended tail. These differing descriptions could mean that several species of all ages exist. Nessie could even be a mother, for two boys once reported seeing tiny, Nessie-like creatures, three feet long, playing in the water around their boat.

People have been startled by Nessie while fishing, boating, or picnicking. Once she nearly overturned a boat by rising up beneath it. People have seen her sunbathing near the shore, walking across the road, splashing and diving for fish, and creating havoc in general.

Some skeptics ask why few sea-monster bones have ever been found. There could be several good reasons for this: Highlanders say the loch never gives up its dead. There is no tide to wash bodies ashore, and strong undercurrents could prevent a body from rising to the surface. Nessie might be unable to float. She might sink like a rock if she were to die. Perhaps sea monsters eat their dead. What if their homes were underwater caverns? There is evidence now showing Loch Ness to be full of ridges and caves. These caverns could be unaffected by currents and monsters could die there and never be found. The waters of Loch Ness are inky black and filled with thick peat moss, making visibility impossible. One diver said it was the most frightening place he had ever dived. In 1976 bones were discovered on the floor of Lake Ness. They indicate a creature with a large massive shape, long neck, and thick tail.

Exactly what kind of creature is Nessie? Could she and her relatives be giant eels, long-necked seals, or huge marine worms, as some have suggested? Or is she kin to the plesiosaur, a marine reptilian creature of the dinosaur age believed extinct for 190 million years?

Since 1934 every trick in the book has been used to catch the mysterious monster, if not in a cage, then at least on film. Some suggested draining the loch or passing an electric current through the water—two very foolish ideas.

34

At one time volunteers were posted all around the lake, making the entire area visible at once. This attempt produced 21 sightings in two weeks; then the weather turned bad, and Nessie is said to hate storms. Once a farmer rigged a boat with an enormous hook and baited it with a dead sheep. For weeks he fished for monsters while everyone laughed. Then one morning his boat was found floating near Urquhart Castle, with the hook still baited. The man had disappeared and no one ever saw him again.

Today another man lives silently at the water's edge, like a hermit. He has been there since 1969, and has seen the monster over twenty-four times and taken eight photographs. There are other men just as dedicated. Some have been lowered into the Ness in cages. Once a small submarine tried to get a good look at Nessie, but the black peaty waters made this impossible. A helicopter with cameras scanned the lake from 3,000 feet in the air (Nessie is afraid of loud noises). Again, there was no cooperation from the monster. Most recently, underwater sonar tracking specialists have explored the depths of the lake. The sonar emits high frequency sounds and collects echoes off of whatever objects they bounce from. These tools are used to detect shipwrecks and downed aircraft. At Loch Ness they detected large moving objects.

Underwater electronic strobe photographs combined with sonar have revealed startling evidence. The sonar tracings showed the passing of two living objects with humps, about 20 to 30 feet long. One photograph showed what was thought to be a fin, 8 feet in length. Another photograph indicated a tail. In 1975, a picture was taken when the monster was only five feet away from the camera. This picture shows what the scientists say are a pair of

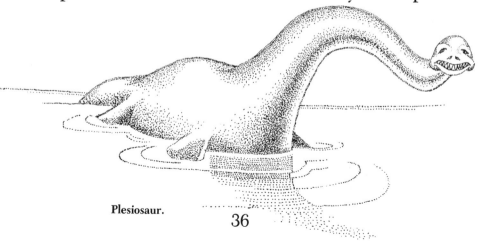

Plesiosaur.

36

horns protruding from the head, flaring nostrils, and a wide open mouth.

Is all this convincing evidence? To many, yes. However, there are always the skeptics. And they believe these photos are only pictures of gas bubbles.

We can only hope that in the very near future scientific evidence will satisfy even the most doubting minds. For after 1400 years of sightings some dictionaries have begun to include Nessie in their pages.

Someday perhaps the right person will come along at the right time, with the right camera, and take the picture that will prove to the world that water monsters really do exist.

THE ABOMINABLE SNOWMAN

One day in 1903, William Knight, an explorer, was wandering in the remote wilderness of the Tibetan plateau. His guides had gone ahead, leaving the Englishman to watch the setting sun alone. As he dismounted his horse, he heard something. And as he turned to look toward the sound, he saw, less than twenty paces away, what may have been an abominable snowman.

He was a little under six feet tall, almost stark naked in that bitter cold—it was the month of November. He was a kind of pale yellow all over . . . a shock of matted hair on his head, little hair on his face, highly splayed (spread out) feet, and large formidable hands. His muscular development in the arms, thighs, legs, and chest was terrific. He had in his hand what seemed to be some form of primitive bow. He did not see me, but stood there, and I watched him for some five or six minutes. So far as I could make out, he was watching some man or beast far down the hillside. At the end of five minutes, he started off at a run down the hill and I was impressed with the tremendous speed at which he travelled.

Knight may well have been the first Western man to see what natives refer to as the Yeti. Yeti means "dweller among the rocks" and is the name given to an unknown beast who frequents the high Himalayas.

In 1921, another English explorer found mysterious tracks. His guides told him that they were imprints of the "wild man of the snows." Excitedly, he sent a telegram to India, attempting to describe, in Nepalese, the "manlike wild creature" he had heard about. The message became garbled and when the telegram reached its destination it read instead, "filthy, dirty or smelly snowman." A newspaper columnist translated this to mean Abominable Snowman. The name was so descriptive that it stuck and has been used ever since.

If Mount Everest was not the highest mountain in the world, and if men had not been so eager to conquer its heights, the Abominable Snowman might still remain virtually unheard of by the Western world.

For a very long time, however, Himalayan tribes have known of the Yeti and feared that he had an appetite for men. Their legends became frightening tales of a monster that stole their yaks (oxen) and their women. They believed the monsters could kill a yak with one blow of their fists. The monsters were thought to be murderers who ran into the mountains to hide, mated there with beasts, and became carnivorous. When hungry they would come down the mountains and steal children. Partial to the tender parts, they were said to only eat the ears, noses and toes of their human victims.

The Sherpa people, brave and famous mountain climbers, warn their children to always run downhill from the Yeti, for his feet are turned backward, and his hair will fall over his face, causing him to trip and fall. Sherpas believe if you look into the face of a Yeti you will surely die.

41

Several expeditions have been organized to search for the Abominable Snowman, but he has proven to be a very elusive creature. However, sightings continue and many footprints have been found. One man discovered what is believed to have been the lair of a snowman, a cave with a nest made of juniper twigs. The branches had been pulled out of the ground, roots and all, an impossible task for a man. Yet the snowmen have been observed often pulling up roots of rhododendron bushes.

There are reports that once a snowman and a snowbaby were captured by a Nepalese tribesman, but no one knows of their fate to this day. A monastery high in the Himalayas prizes what it claims to be the mummified hand and hair-covered skull of a Yeti. The monks will not permit these relics to leave their sanctuary however. Once in 1952, a black tuft of bristly hair was found on a rocky ledge during a hunting expedition. The Sherpas accompanying the hunters said it was Yeti hair. They immediately became very nervous and said it would be bad luck to keep the hair because it would make the snowman angry at their people. One of the Sherpas grabbed the evidence and threw it over a cliff.

Some skeptics say the Abominable Snowman is nothing more than a langur monkey or a Tibetan blue bear, an animal so rare that it has never been seen alive or hunted down by Western man. Others definitely believe that the Yeti is real, for they have seen it. They speak of it as being a stooped, hairy creature, shaggy and very muscular. Its eyes are close set and sunken and the head is pointed at the top. Its cry is mewing, catlike. Sometimes it makes a shrill whistle. The animal seems to move about mostly at night and lives on plants and small animals of the highest mountain pastures. It is thought to feed mainly on mouse hares, small animals that live in rocky crevices at the highest altitudes, for fresh remains of mouse hare have been found simultaneously with the sighting of a Yeti indicating the beast removed the entrails before eating, a trait that is strikingly human.

Those who climb Everest brave many hazards. There are literally swarms of leeches and locusts to contend with. Treacherous swinging bridges provide the only passage over deep mountain gorges. Climbers may suffer from altitude sickness, frostbite, and sunstroke, all at the same time. They have to cross some of the world's most damp regions, and areas where rain constantly falls. The air is so thin and cold at the summit of Everest it seems impossible that any animal could survive. Yet the mysterious tracks of the abominable snowpeople have been found, even there.

On the other side of the Himalayas, the Soviet side, Russian citizens say they also have seen horrible, hairy, two-legged beasts. They are called Almas, or wild men, and haunt the slopes of the Pamir mountains. Local natives believe they are very mischievous for these people are always missing some of their pots and pans, or even their laundry, which usually reappears some days later, hanging from the craggy edge of a cliff, blowing in the breeze. They believe the Alma sleeps in a crouched position, resting on his knees, with his head covered by his hands. One Russian scientist believed that the snowmen were surviving remnants of Neanderthal man, driven centuries ago into the more inhospitable parts of Central Asia. Chinese manuscripts, dating back to 200 B. C. depict creatures resembling the Yeti or Alma. Some experts believe there may be four different species living in different parts of the world.

In 1941, a Russian army doctor, stationed in the Caucasus, was called to a nearby village to look after a "wild man" who had just been captured. The man was less than six feet in height and fully covered with dark brown hair, except for his face. He was ridden with lice and exuded a strong, foul stench. The naked wild man was uncomfortable indoors and sweated profusely, even in the low heat of the barn in which he was being held captive. The creature was inarticulate, emitting only "bull-like sounds." His eyes had an empty, animal-like expression.

The army doctor decided that the creature was some kind of primitive man. No one knows what happened to the Alma, however. One account said he escaped; another said he was shot by a firing squad, a fate heard to have been suffered by other such creatures in those regions.

In 1964, a Mongolian scientist declared that the Almas had been squeezed into an area about 385 miles square. Most people who live near the habitat of snowmen agree that their numbers are becoming fewer and fewer. We can only hope that this truly exciting animal will not disappear from our earth before we can prove its existence and save it from extinction.

BIG FOOT

Indians of the West Coast have
many legends about the "wild man
of the woods." The Kwakiutl
tribes of British Columbia called
him Buquis. They believed he was
a giant man-eater and carved scary
wooden masks of his face. Their
legend describes the Buquis
monster as having a "whistling
breath." Denna Indians also
believed in a hairy man-like giant,
whom they called Gilyuk. They
too feared

that Gilyuk ate people. Indians of Washington and Oregon believed a tribe of wild men called Selatiks lived in their mountains. And the Seminoles of Florida also spoke of such a creature. The Chepalis, near Vancouver, believed the monsters were descendants of a race of giants almost exterminated in battle many years ago. The Spokane Indians of northern Washington feared men-stealing giants that inhabited a certain snow-covered mountain. A missionary to these people compared their descriptions of the giants to a biblical account of such a race of beings. These Indians spoke of the strong smell of the beasts, their whistling calls, and said that they would often throw rocks at their houses in the night.

For hundreds of years North American Indians have known the "wild man of the woods."

We now believe it possible that such creatures inhabit wilderness areas on five continents. They are called by many names and many stories are told about them. In

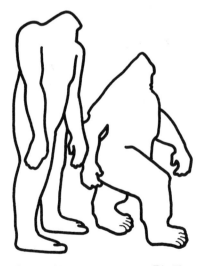

Abominable Snowman.   Big Foot.

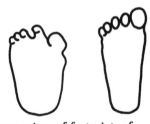

Comparison of footprints of
Abominable Snowman and Big Foot.

48

South America the creature is known as Momo Grande (Big Man) or Hombre de la Nieve (Man of the Snow). Indians of Ecuador and Nicaragua believe these creatures inhabit remote mountains of their jungles. In the seventeenth century Spanish gold hunters supposedly shot and killed fourteen of the mystery animals. In Canada and British Columbia the most common name for them is Karakawa, or Sasquatch (hairy men). But most of the United States has adopted the Rocky Mountain Indian's favorite name for the monster—Big Foot.

Men-animals have been sighted in many areas of the United States. Most often they are seen in the Cascade Mountains of Washington, Oregon, and Northern California. Recently, however, Big Feet have been sighted in the Mojave Desert. People also claim to have seen the hairy giants in the Everglades of Florida, the Blue Ridge Mountains of Arkansas, the bogs of Louisiana, and in most of the fifty states. People have seen Big Feet standing by roadsides, swimming in lakes, wading in rivers, eating berries from bushes, and watching them from the edge of the woods.

What may have been a young Big Foot was captured near Yale, British Columbia, by some railroad men in 1884. He was put in a cage and named Jacko. Nobody knows what became of Jacko. He may have died or have been sold to a circus. His captor had planned to take him to London to exhibit him according to the only newspaper account we have of the story.

Another man, while prospecting in 1924, claimed he was kidnapped by a family of Big Feet. They carried him off in a sleeping bag and kept him prisoner for six days. They did not harm him but were very curious and extremely shy. The prospector finally managed to trick the "old man" Big Foot into eating a packet full of snuff. When he became violently ill, the man ran for his life. The "old lady" Big Foot gave chase but he managed to escape her. For many years the prospector told no one of his experience, fearing he would be ridiculed.

Another man said he once shot an ape-like creature. That night and for several nights thereafter, he and his companions were bombarded by rocks as they sought refuge in their cabin. Today, in the Big Foot territory of the Pacific Northwest there are at least four sightings of the animal every year.

So many accounts by eyewitnesses would seem to prove that Big Foot is not just a legend. However, evidence of other kinds also point to his existence. Thousands of footprints have been found and many of them made into plaster casts. Tape recordings of his voice have been analyzed by computers. They seem to indicate an animal about nine feet in height, who can articulate better than an ape but not as well as a man. Samples of hair have been found that did not belong to any known animal. The Smithsonian was unable to positively identify hair samples which have been sent to them and represented as having come from a Big Foot creature. In 1974 a sample of hair was presented to a microbiologist in Portland, Oregon. The hair was labeled as "humanoid, but not human." Fecal material, resembling that of humans, has been found near Big Foot's tracks. Several photographs and motion pictures have also been taken of the ape people.

Some Big Feet have been sighted that were over six feet tall; others seemed to be closer to ten feet. Eyewitnesses believe the animals to weigh between 400 to 800 pounds. He is said to have a wide mouth and square teeth. His eyes glow and are shadowed by heavy brows. Big Foot is hairy all over except for the palms of his hands and soles of his feet. His face has little or no hair. When you touch the bristly hair, it pricks like needles. The creature walks stoop-shouldered and has no tail. He is said to be a foxy red or blackish color. The accompanying chart shows Big Foot's size compared to that of a man, a bear, and an ape.

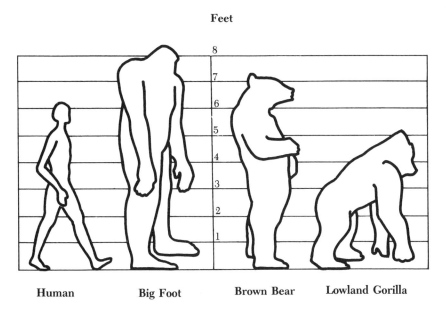

Feet

Human   Big Foot   Brown Bear   Lowland Gorilla

Many believe the monster is only a big bear. And indeed brown bears can grow to be ten feet tall and weigh over 1700 pounds. But bears walk on all four feet most of the time, while Big Foot walks upright, on two feet like a man. And, unlike a bear, Big Foot has no snout. Some say his face is leathery. Most say it is ape-like.

The tracks of Big Foot are not like bear tracks. He has five toes and no claws—a footprint that looks very much like a man's. This illustration shows the size of a Big Foot's track in comparison to the track of a man and a gorilla. The

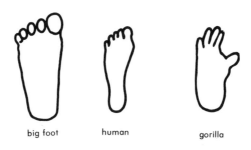

big foot   human   gorilla

Tracks of Big Foot, human, gorilla.

largest tracks have been found in the state of Washington—tracks that measured 23 inches long. However, the average size of his footprint is between 14 and 17 inches in length.

Big Foot has been heard to chatter in a sort of half laugh, half language. His voice has also been described as sounding similar to the cry of a seagull. People often hear him make a yelping cry like that of an ape, a cry that ends in a whistle. Indians believed that these whistling sounds were really bird calls.

Experts believe Big Foot lives in caves and eats mostly mice, plants, and berries. However, in wintertime when vegetation is scarce, people claim they have seen him tear apart sheep and deer with his bare hands.

Few people have ever seen Big Foot hurt humans. They seem to be gentle beasts who want only to be left alone. But they have been known to throw rocks at people or to attack those who shoot at them or at other Big Feet. In Skamania County, Washington, it is against the law to kill these hairy giants, and Oregon also passed such a law in 1977.

Big Foot has a horrible smell. People say it is an odor so foul you will never forget it once you have been near the animal. Some describe it as musky, some say it is a wild beast smell, and others have compared it to the smell of sulphur, rotten eggs, or decaying meat. Big Foot smells so bad that in Florida they call him the Skunk Ape.

Anthropologists are scientists who study man. Some of these scientists do not believe in Big Foot at all. Others think he is either a man-ape, an advanced form of the prehistoric gigantopithecus, or an ape-man, like the Neanderthal or Peking man. There are many traits shared between prehistoric man and our mysterious creature.

Gigantopithecas, the largest primate that ever lived.

Peking man, a primitive man of about 475,000 B.C.

Cavemen had heavy brows. So does Big Foot. Their footprints are similar. Cavemen removed the intestines of animals before eating them. Big Foot and the Yeti have been known to do the same thing. Cavemen made weapons. The abominable snowman was once seen carrying a primitive bow. Cavemen buried their dead. One eyewitness claimed to have seen three Big Feet doing just that. He saw them dig a large hole with their hands, place their dead companion in the grave, and cover him with 300 pound boulders. More than once bodies have mysteriously disappeared of the few Big Feet reportedly killed in the wilderness. This leads us to believe that companions may have carried away their corpses.

Skeptics say people who believe they are seeing Big Foot are really only seeing a big bear or a tree stump. They think Big Foot exists only in our imagination. Could it be possible that people on every continent except Australia,

for hundreds of years, all have had such similar imaginations? Why are these "imaginary" creatures always described as being half-man, half-beast, or ape-like men, or man-like hairy giants, or men-animals? Eyewitnesses often tell of their surprise at seeing the creature wearing no clothes. Would we expect to see a gorilla in trousers? Why then does it seem so strange to see a naked Big Foot? Is it because they are so very man-like? Would an "imaginary" animal the size of Big Foot be expected to roar ferociously and behave in a violent manner, or would he be described as a whistling giant, shy and gentle, with the voice of a seagull? And would a monster of such proportions throw only rocks at his enemies?

If these creatures originated in Asia, as some believe, then how did Big Foot get to North America? He may have migrated millions of years ago by what was once the Bering Strait land bridge (connecting Russia to Alaska). Once here, there were plenty of places for him to hide, for at least 10 percent of the earth is still unexplored, and finding him is like trying to find a needle in a haystack, a moving needle. On the North American continent alone there are 250,000 square miles of wilderness in British Columbia (with only one main road), 17,000 square miles in Oregon, where nobody lives, and a wilderness in California about the size of Maine.

Western man spends much time speculating about who or what Big Foot could be. Indians were more concerned with why he was here. And although some tribes feared him and believed him a cannibal, they all respected him.

The Yurok Indians of California regarded him with kindness. He was the original environmentalist, their protector . . . a creature put on earth by God to keep man and nature in harmony. What do you believe?

Kwakiutl mask representing the Wild Man of the Woods. The original is in the National Museum of Canada, Ottawa.

READING LIST

Bartsch "The Squid and Octopus." Smithsonian Institution Annual Report, pp. 361–72. Washington, D. C.: Library of Congress, 1916.

Baumann, Elwood D. *The Loch Ness Monster.* New York: Franklin Watts, Inc., 1972.

Burden, W. Douglas. *Dragon Lizards of Komodo.* New York: G. P. Putnam's Sons, 1927.

Burton, Dr. Maurice and Robert Burton (general editors). *The International Wildlife Encyclopedia*, pp. 921–23, 1257. New York: Marshall Cavendish Corporation, 1969.

Byrne, Peter. *Big Foot.* Washington, D. C.: Acropolis Books Ltd., 1975.

Chester, Michael. *Water Monsters*, p. 29. New York: Grosset & Dunlap., Inc., 1973.

Cook, Joseph J. and William L. Wisner. *The Phantom World of the Octopus and Squid*, pp. 37–49. New York: Dodd, Mead & Co., 1965.

Costello, Peter. *In Search of Lake Monsters.* London: Garnstone Press Ltd., 1974.

DuBerrie, Jeuan. *I Lived With Gorilla.* London: Stanley Paul & Co. Ltd., 1937.

Green, John. *On the Track of the Sasquatch.* Agassiz, British Columbia: Cheam Publishing Ltd., 1968.

———— *1970 Year of the Sasquatch.* Agassiz, British Columbia: Cheam Publishing Ltd., 1970.

———— *1973, The Sasquatch File.* Agassiz, British Columbia: Cheam Publishing Ltd., 1973.

Guenette, Robert and Frances. *Bigfoot: The Mysterious Monster.* Los Angeles: Schick Sun Classic Pictures, 1975.

Harrison, George H. "On the Trail of Bigfoot." *National Wildlife Magazine* (John Strohn, ed.), Vol. 8, No. 6 (October–November, 1970), pp. 4–9.

Izzard, Ralph. *The Abominable Snowman*. New York: Doubleday & Co., Inc., 1955

Kay, Helen. *Apes*. pp. 4–5, 14. New York: Macmillan, Inc., 1970.

Kern, James A. "Dragon Lizards of Komodo." *National Geographic Magazine* (Melville Bell Grosvenor, ed. in chief), Vol. 134, No. 6 (December, 1968), pp. 872–80.

Knowlton, William. *Sea Monsters*. New York: Alfred A. Knopf, 1959.

Laycock, George. *Strange Monsters and Great Searches*. p. 67. Garden City, N.Y.: Doubleday & Co., Inc., 1973.

Lemmon, Robert S. *All About Strange Beasts of the Present*. New York: Random House, 1957.

Mackie, John Duncan, *A History of Scotland*. New York: Penguin, 1964.

O'Toole, Thomas. "Scientists to Return to Loch Ness." *The Washington Post*, April 19, 1976, p. A9.

Place, Marion Templeton. *On the Track of Big Foot*. New York: Dodd, Mead & Co., 1974.

Schaller, George S. *The Mountain Gorilla*. Chicago: University of Chicago Press, 1963.

Snaith, Stanley. *At Grips With Everest*. New York: Oxford University Press, 1938.

Soule, Gardner. *The Maybe Monsters*. New York: G. P. Putnam's Sons, 1963.

———— *Trail of the Abominable Snowman*. New York: G. P. Putnam's Sons, 1966.

"South Pacific Nessie." *Newsweek* magazine. August 1, 1977, p. 77.

Stonor, Charles. *The Sherpa and the Snowman*. London: Hollis and Carter, 1955.

Sweeney, James B. *A Pictorial History of Sea Monsters and Other Dangerous Marine Life*. New York: Crown Publishers, Inc., 1972.

Wild Wild World of Animals: "Elephants and Other Land Giants." Time-Life Films, 1976.